Fuck It

By Owen McDaniel

A swear word coloring book.

With 24 illustrations for hours of fun stress relieving!

This book is designed to help relieve stress because sometimes you just have to say fuck it and color on!

Be sure to check us out on Facebook and our website for other great things!

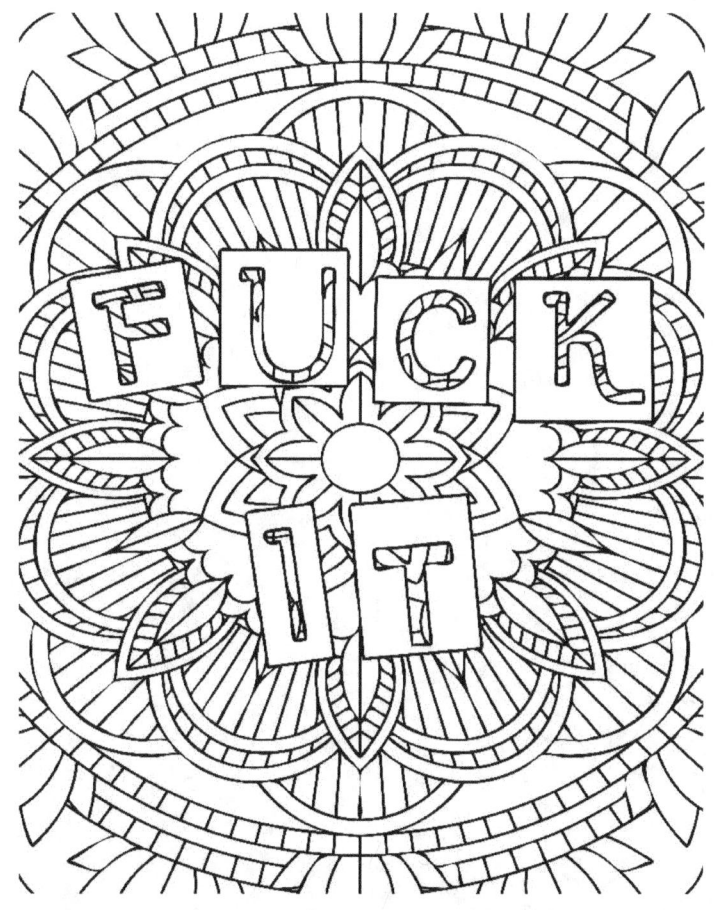

http://mcdanielcoloringbooks.weebly.com

https://www.facebook.com/McDanielColoringBooks

Images in this book are created from original art work. Copyright 2017 Owen McDaniel. All rights reserved.

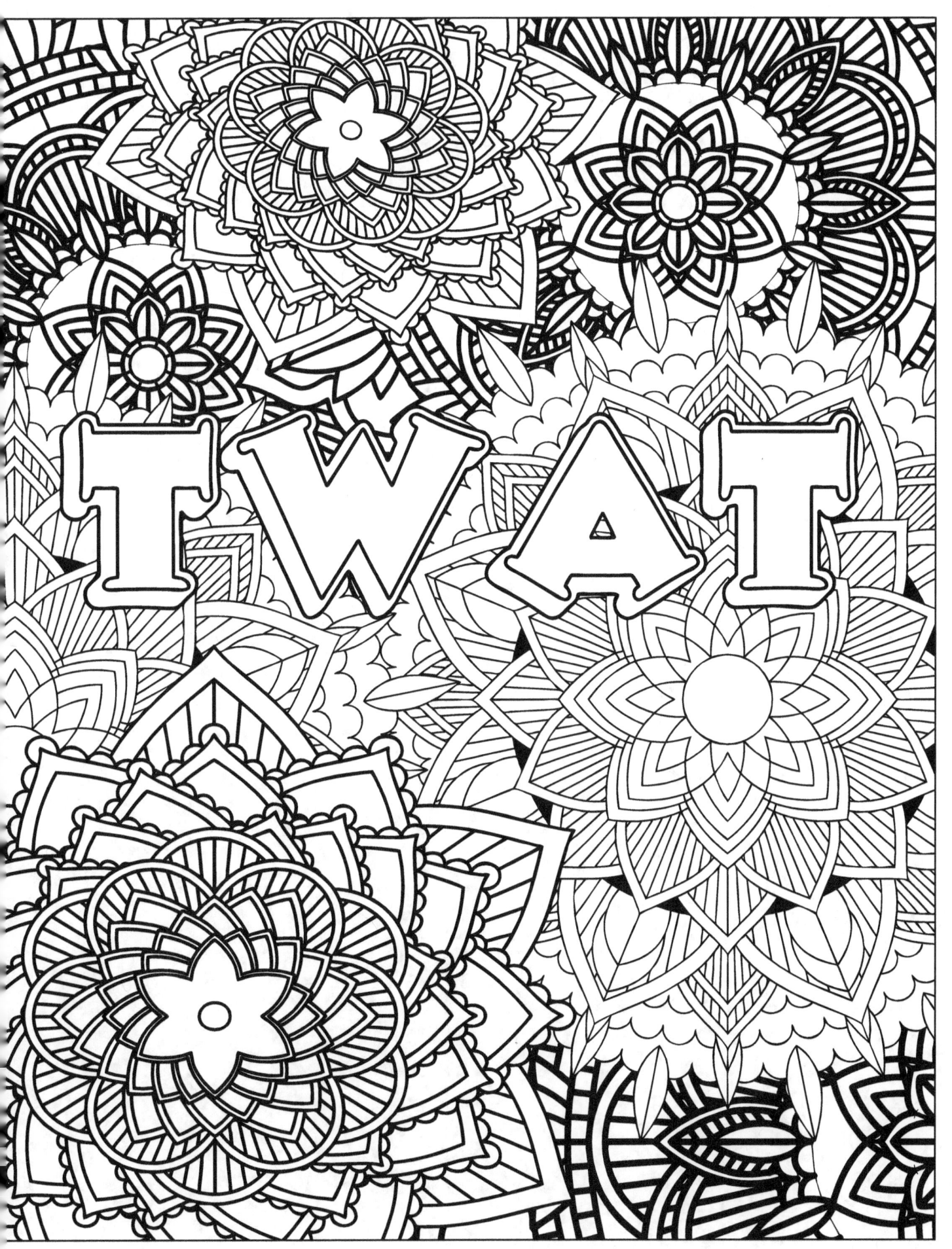

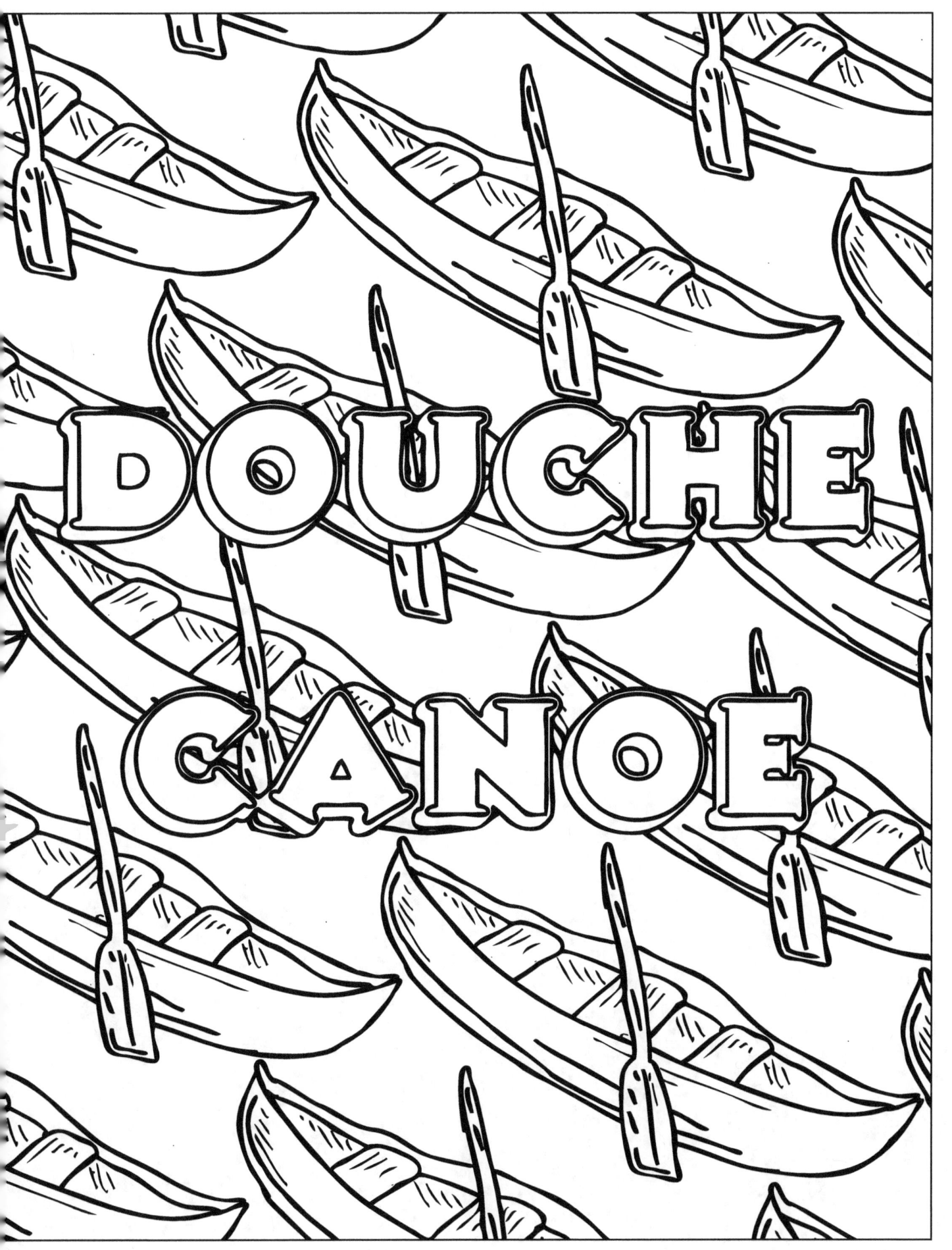

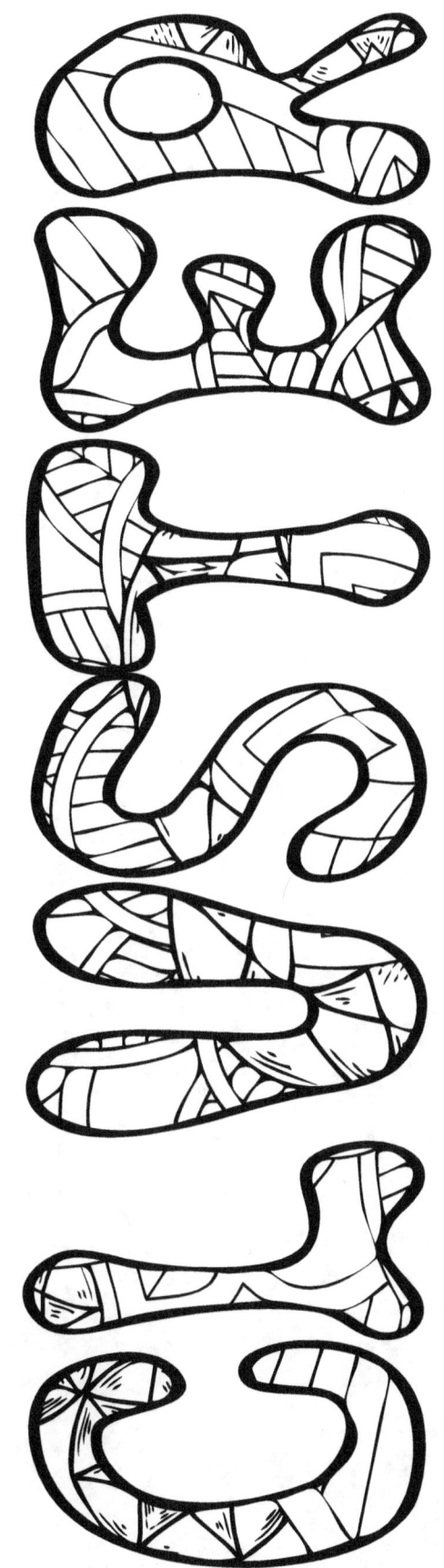
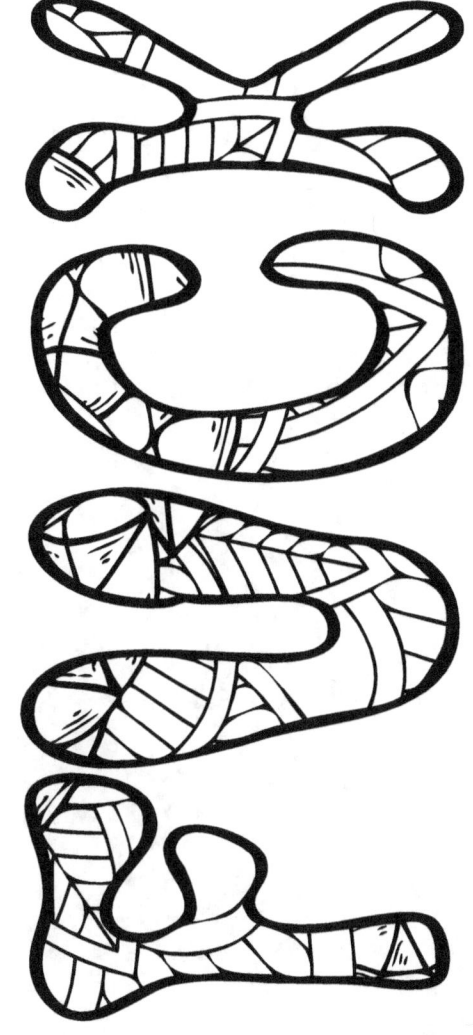

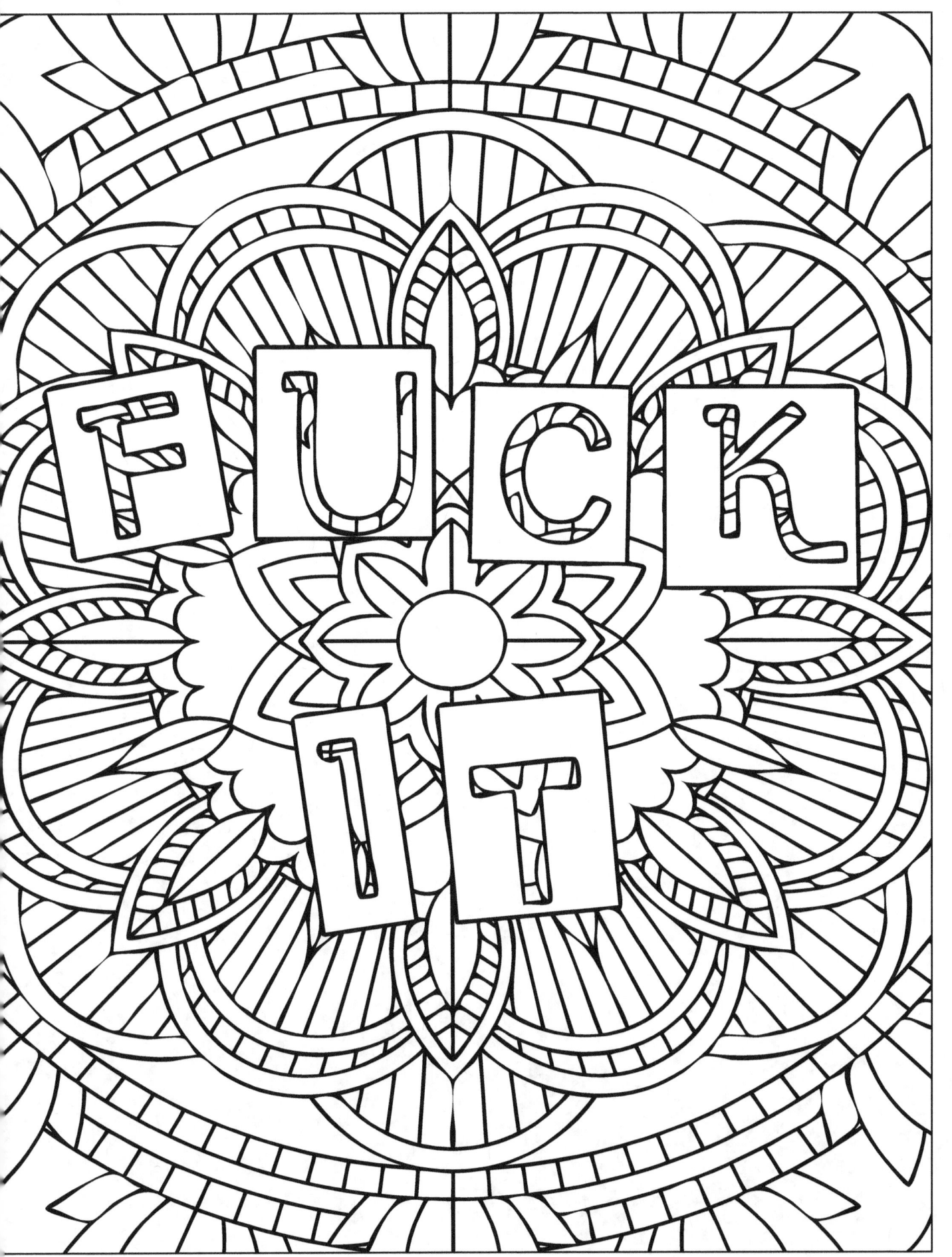

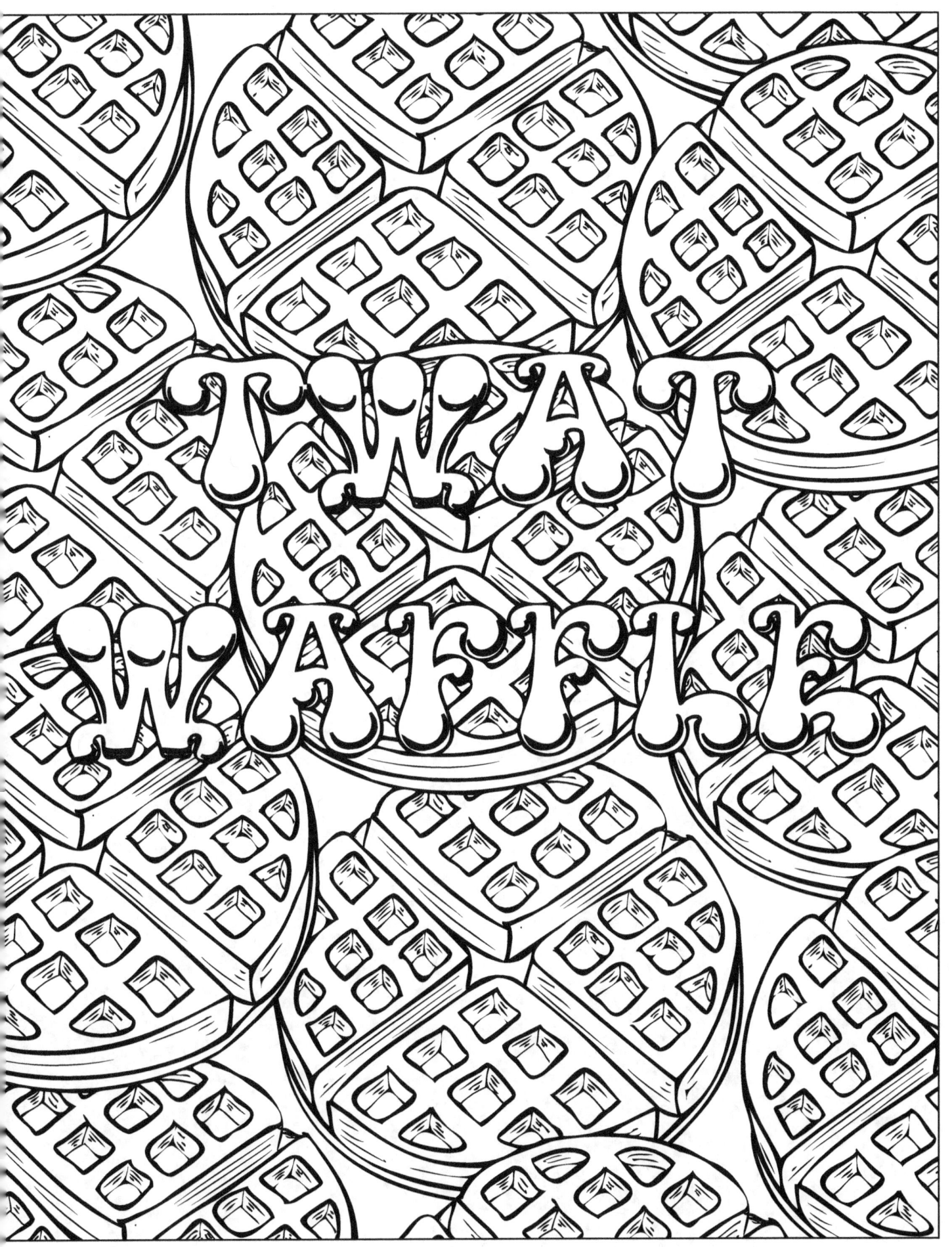

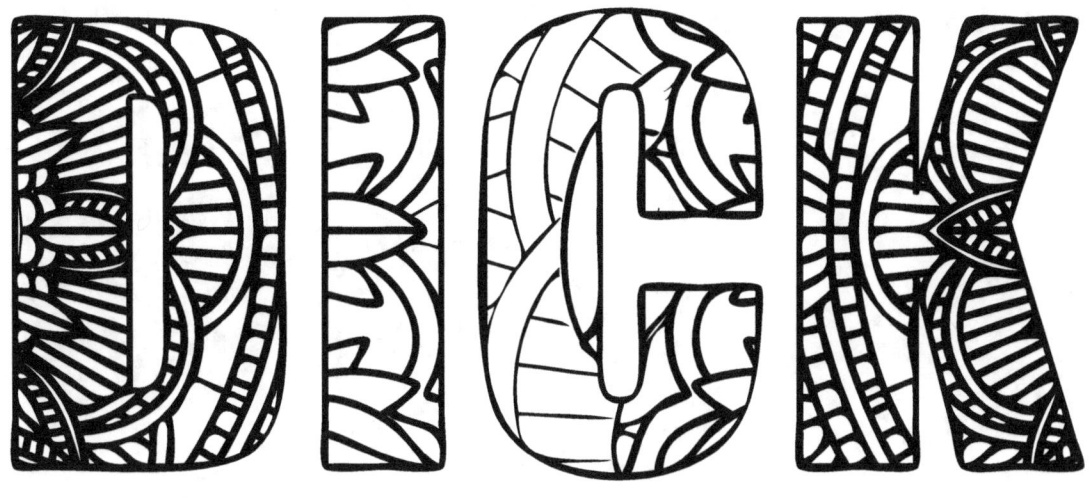
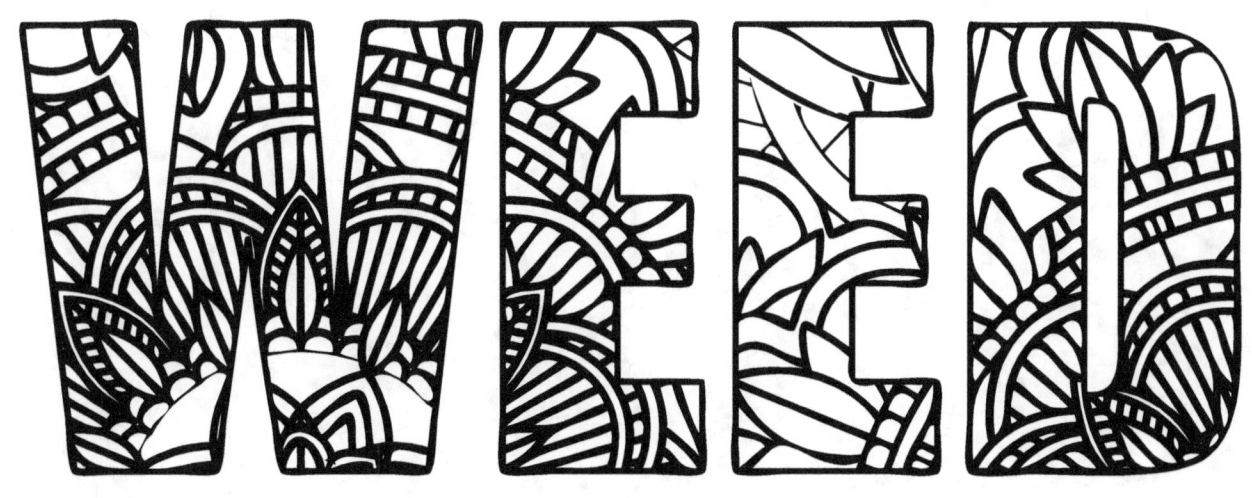

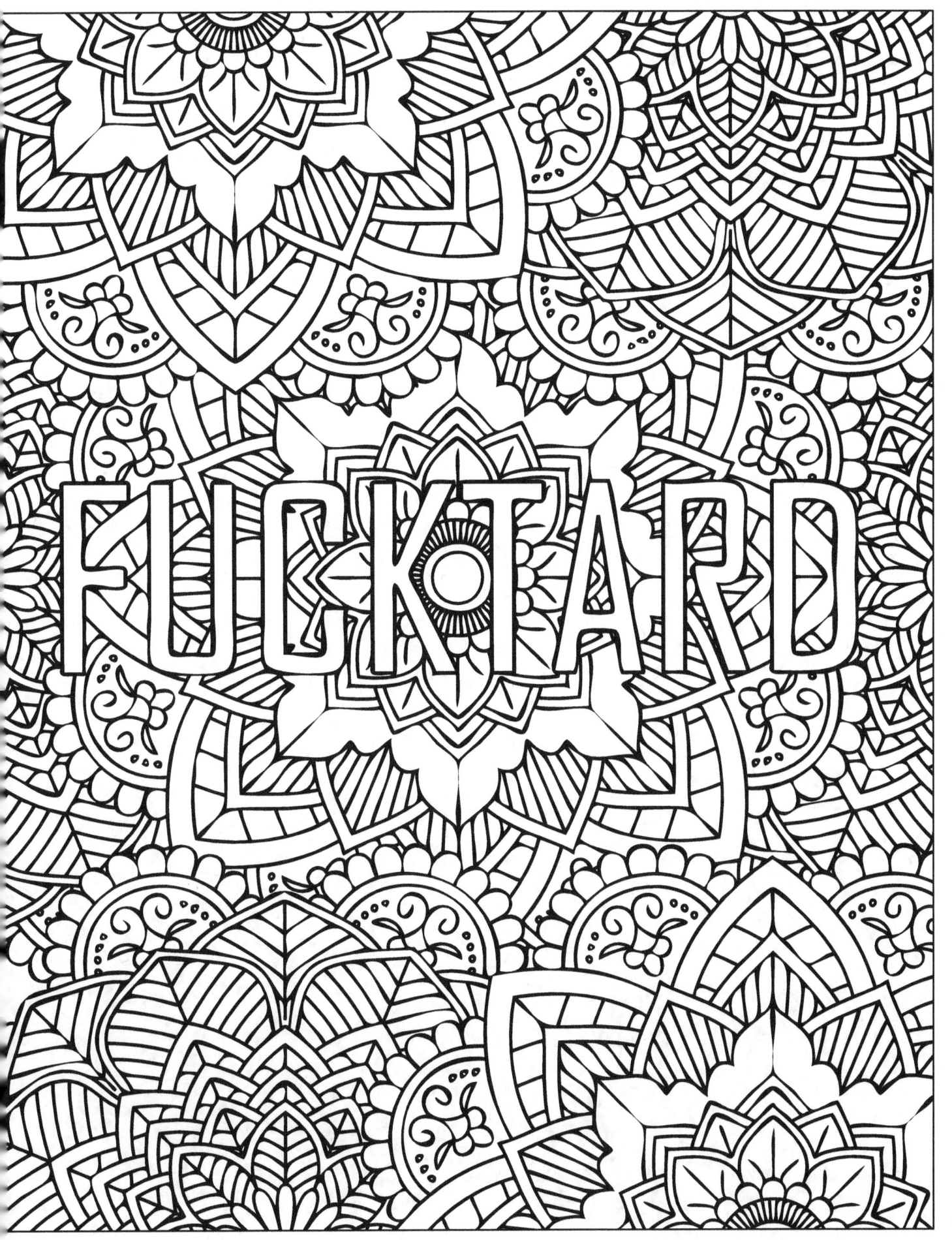

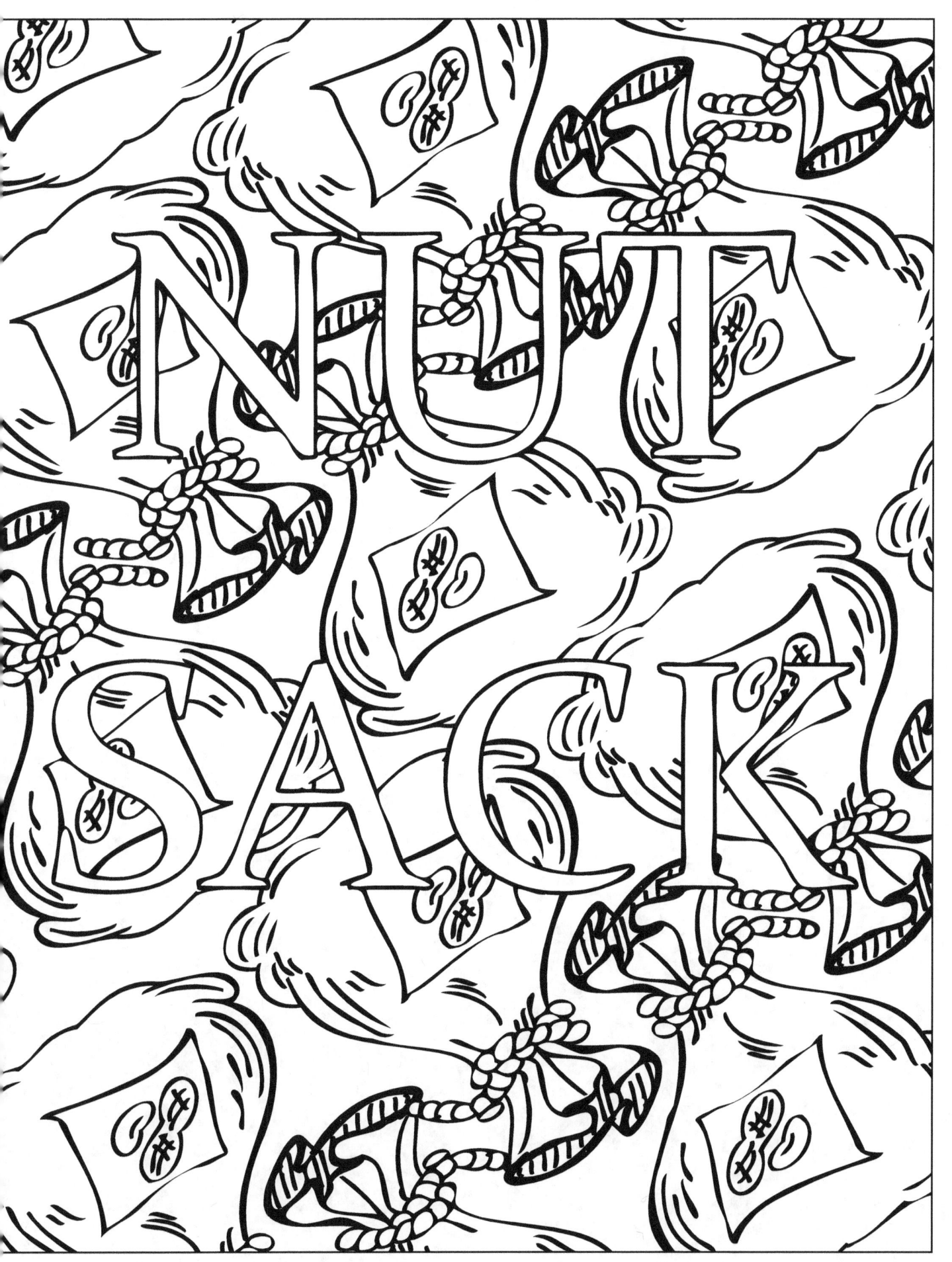

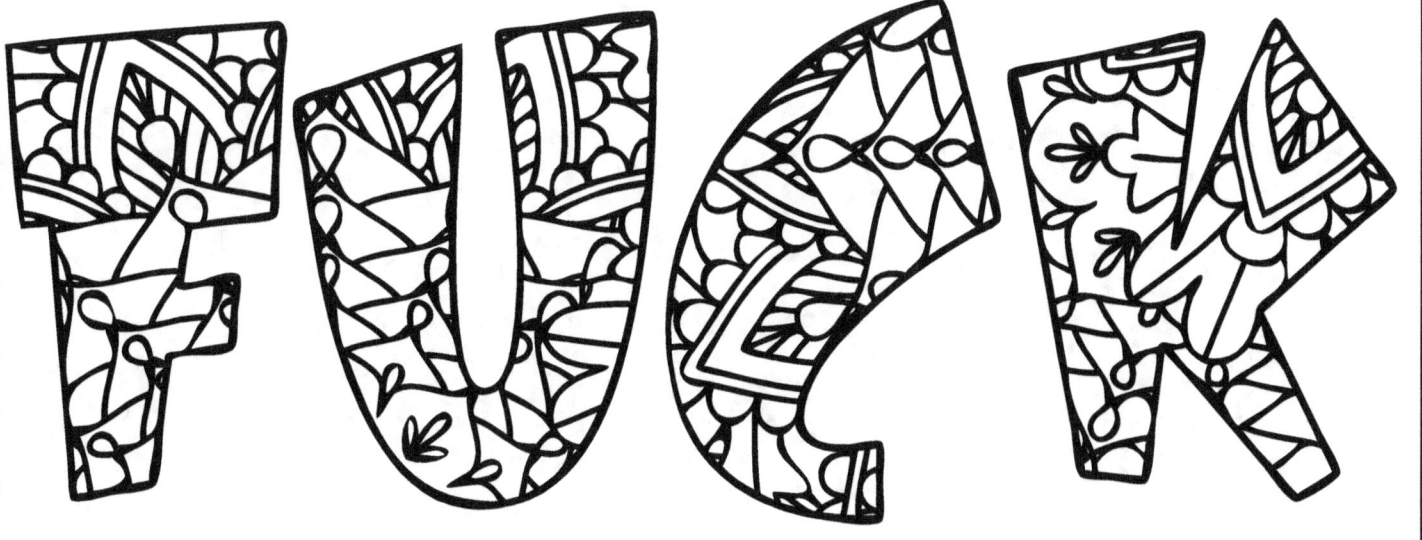

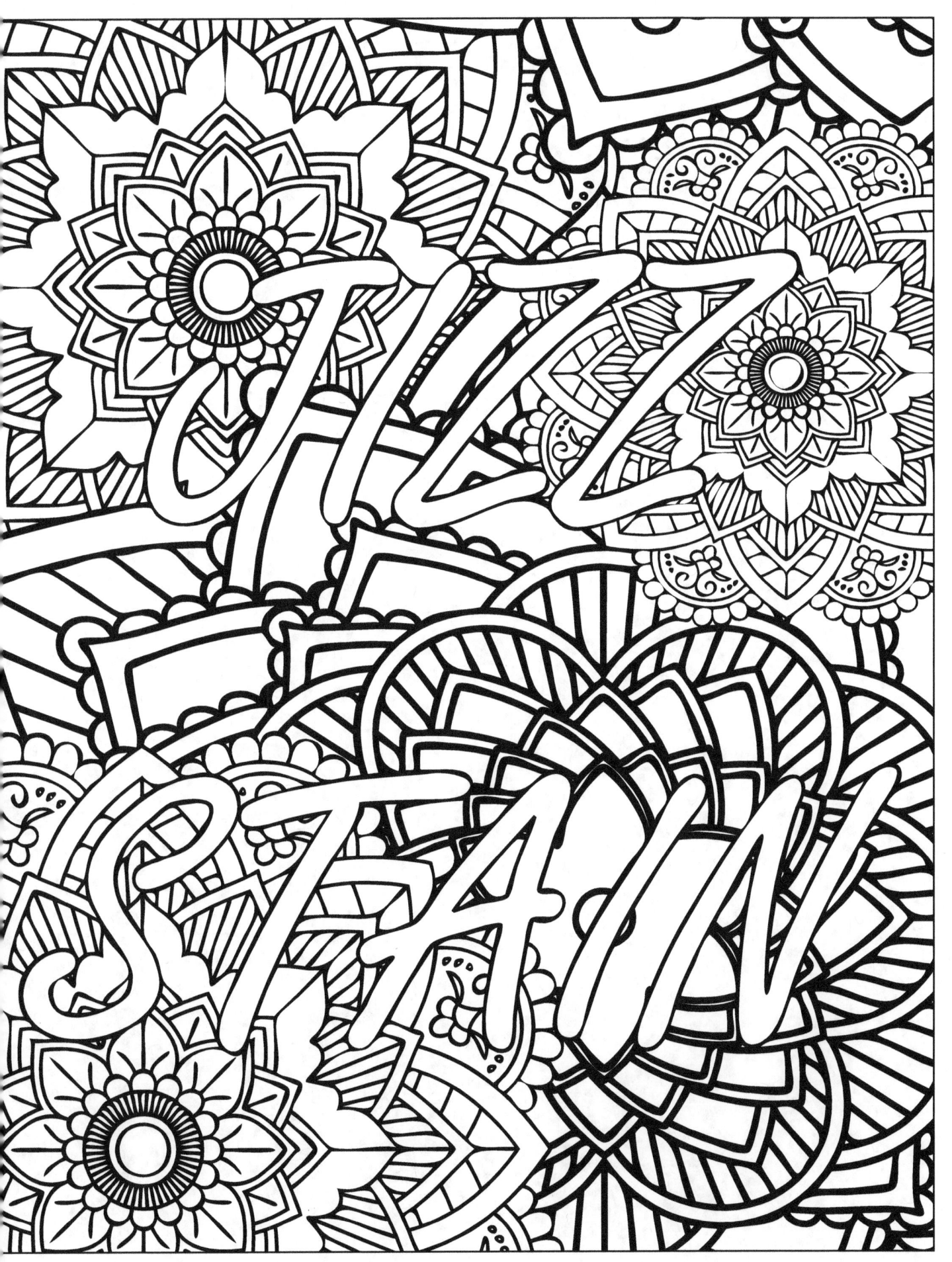

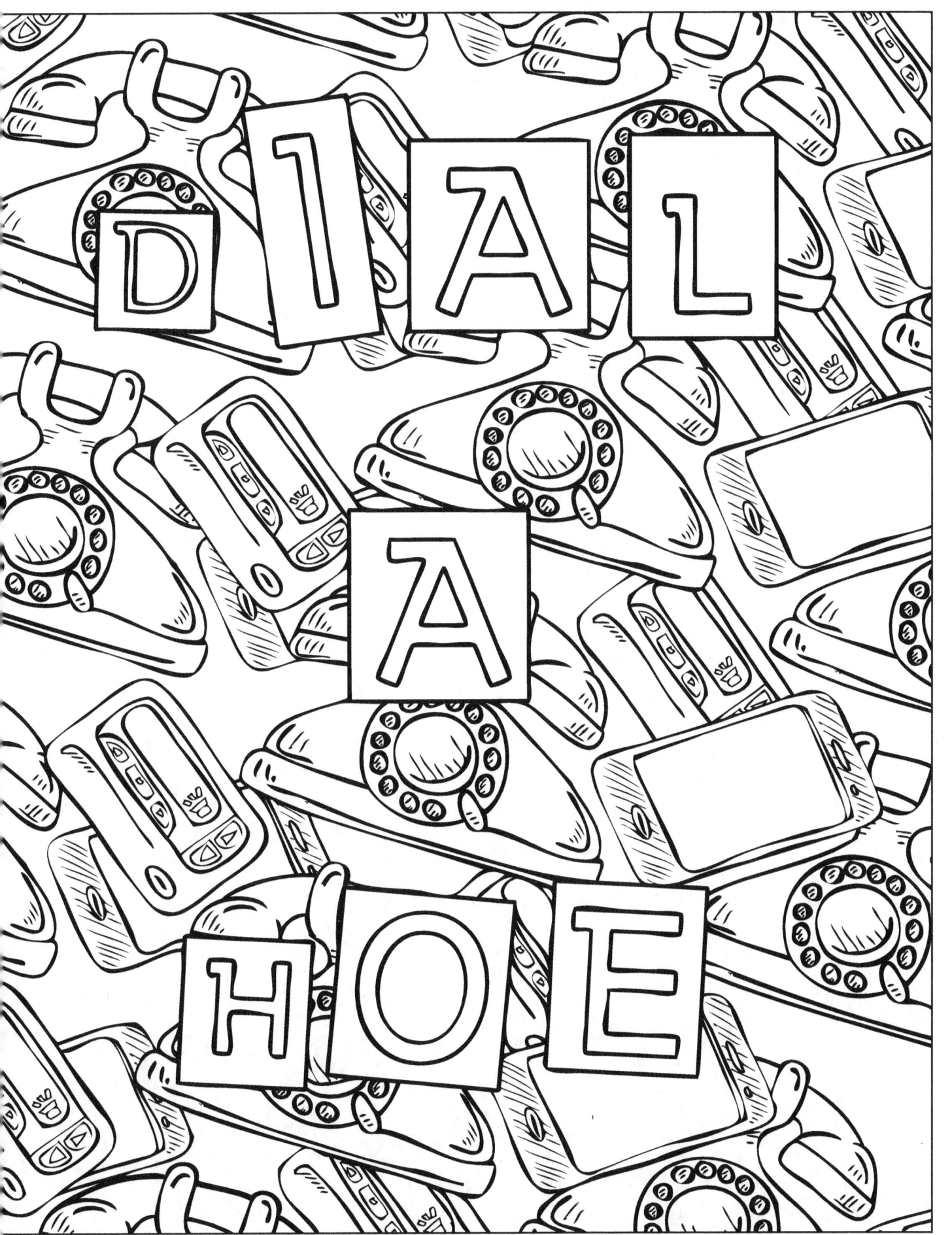

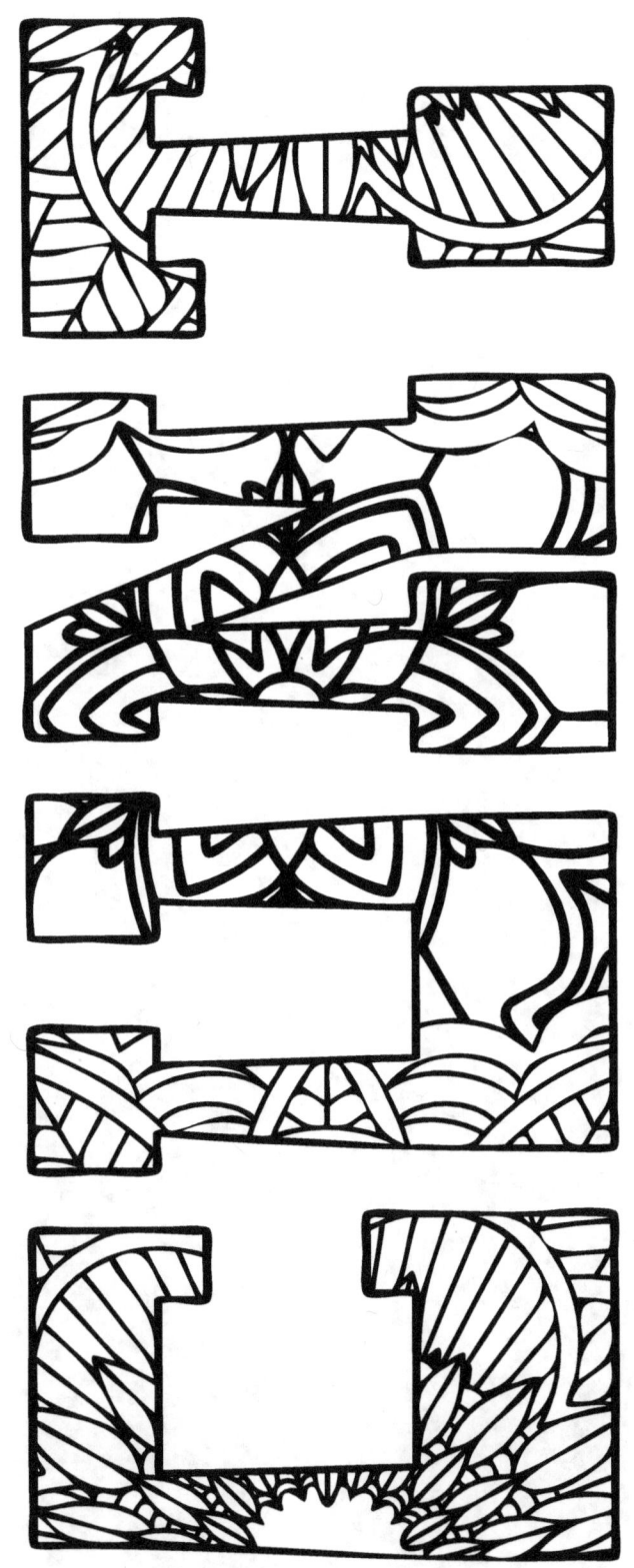

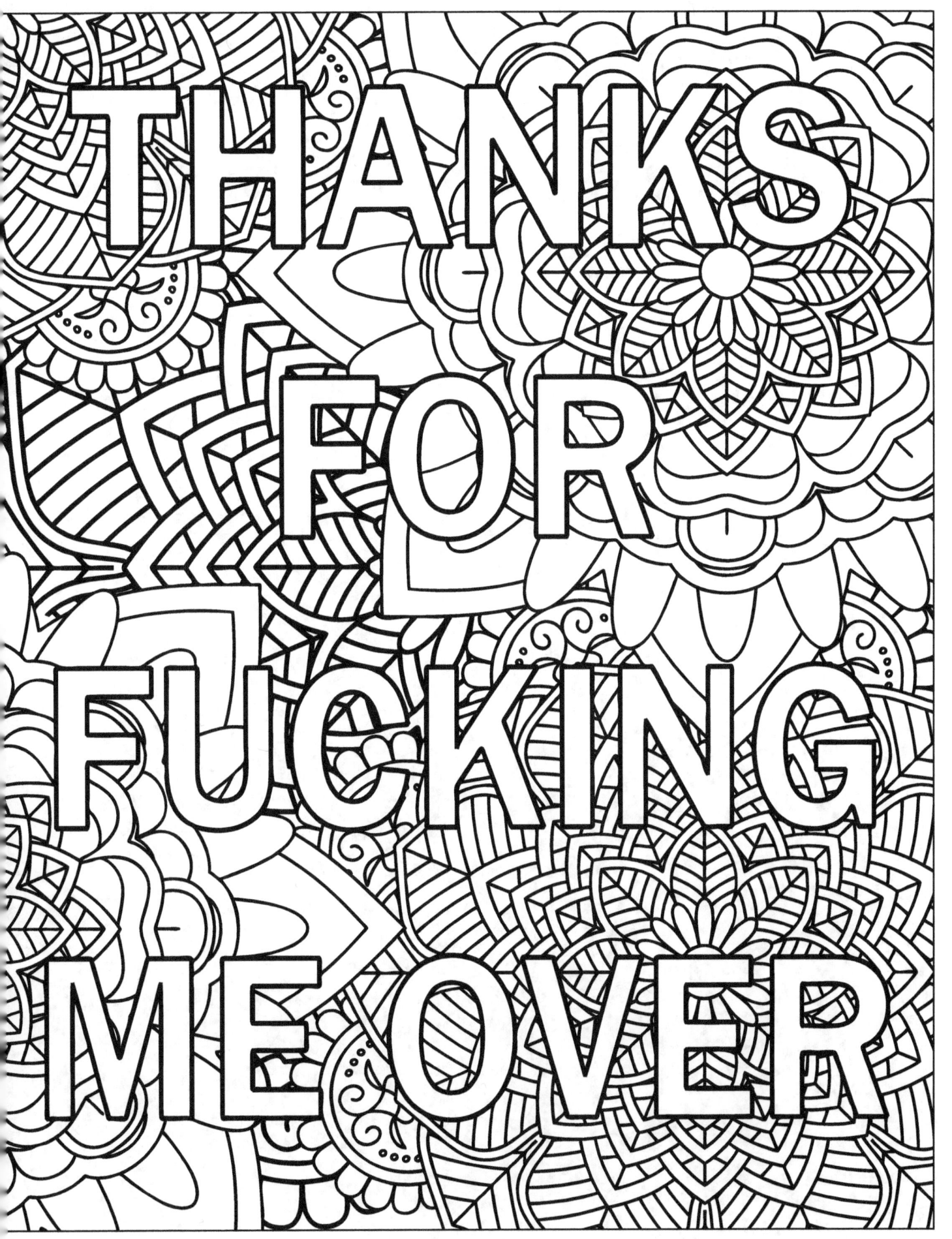

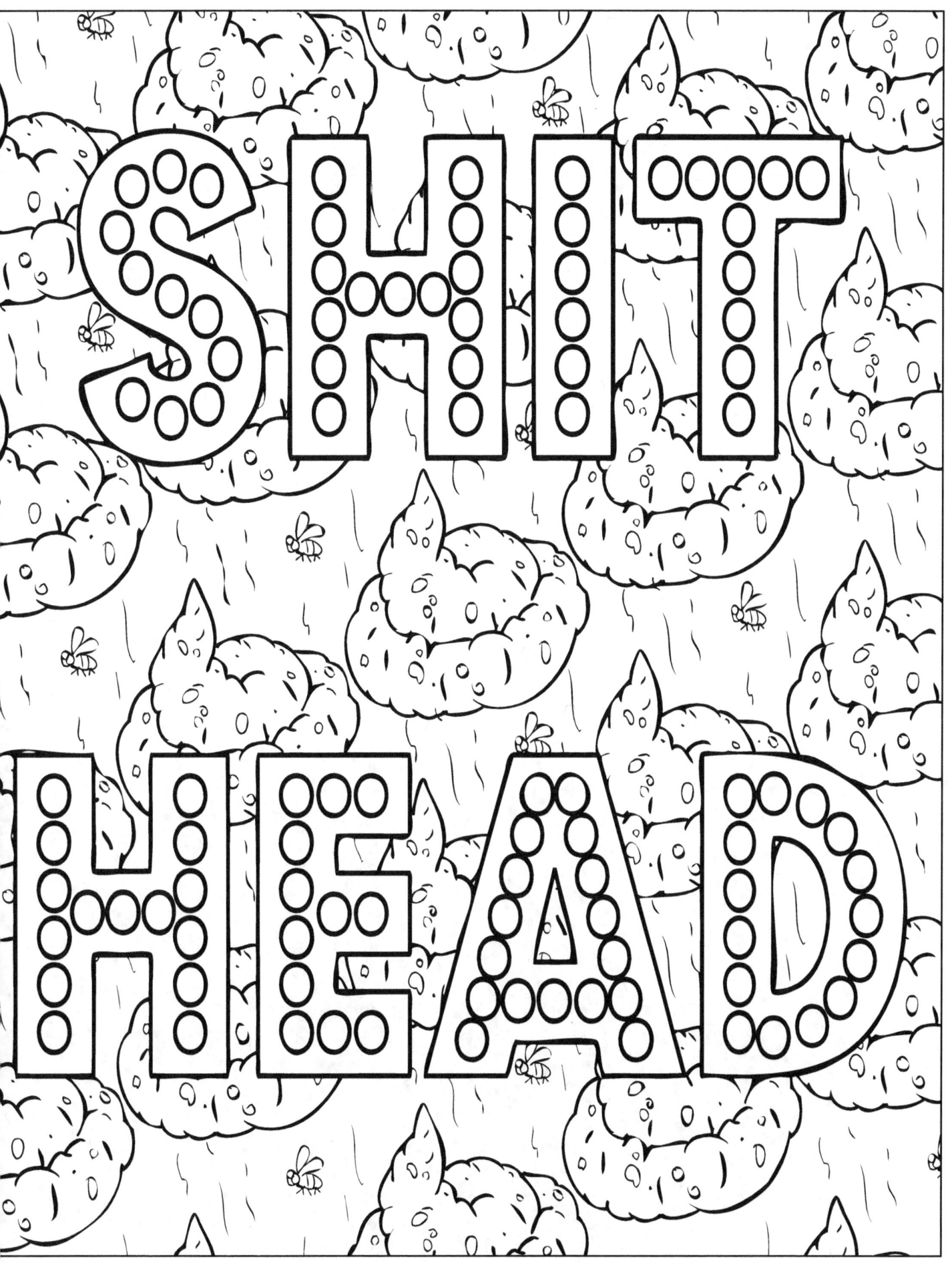

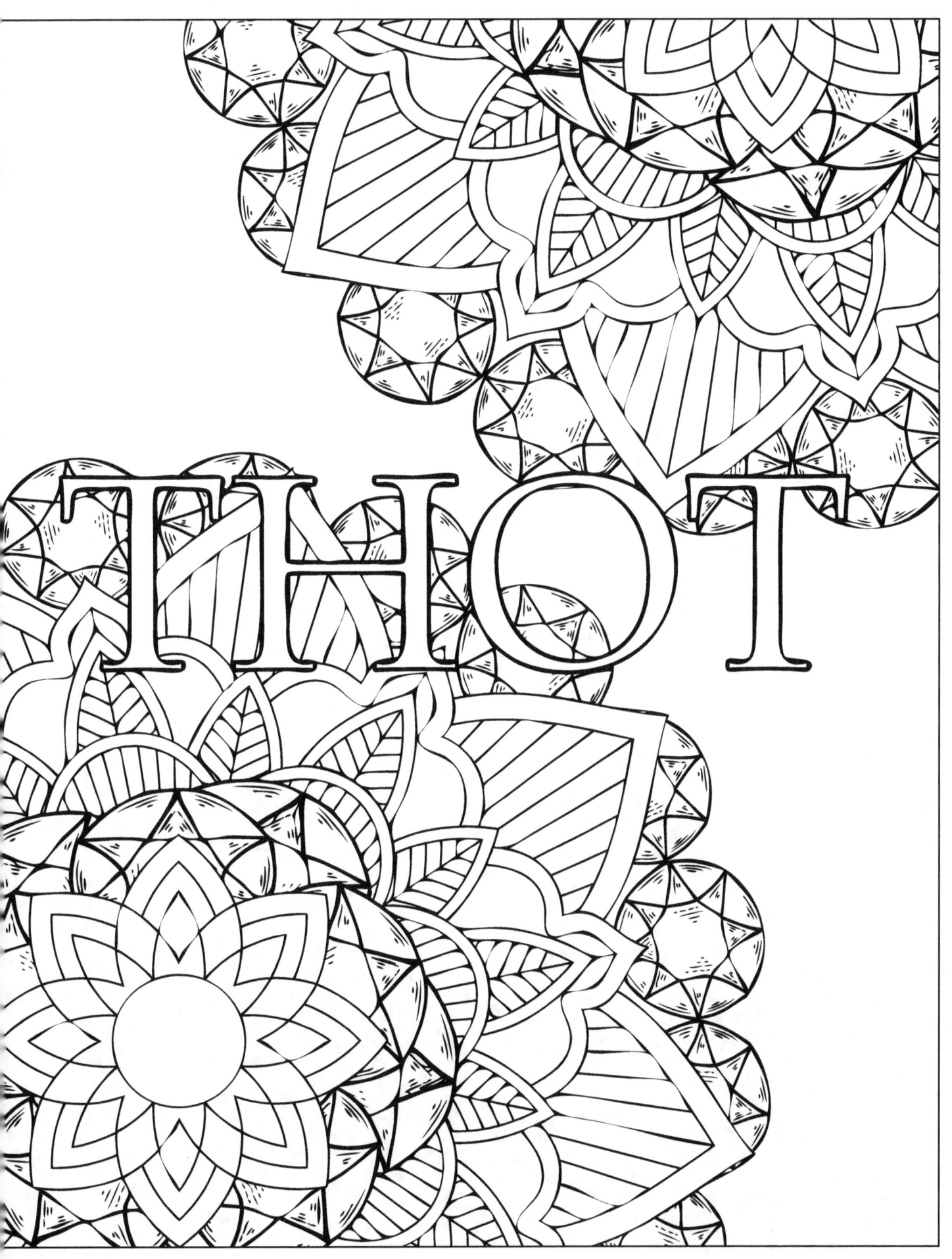

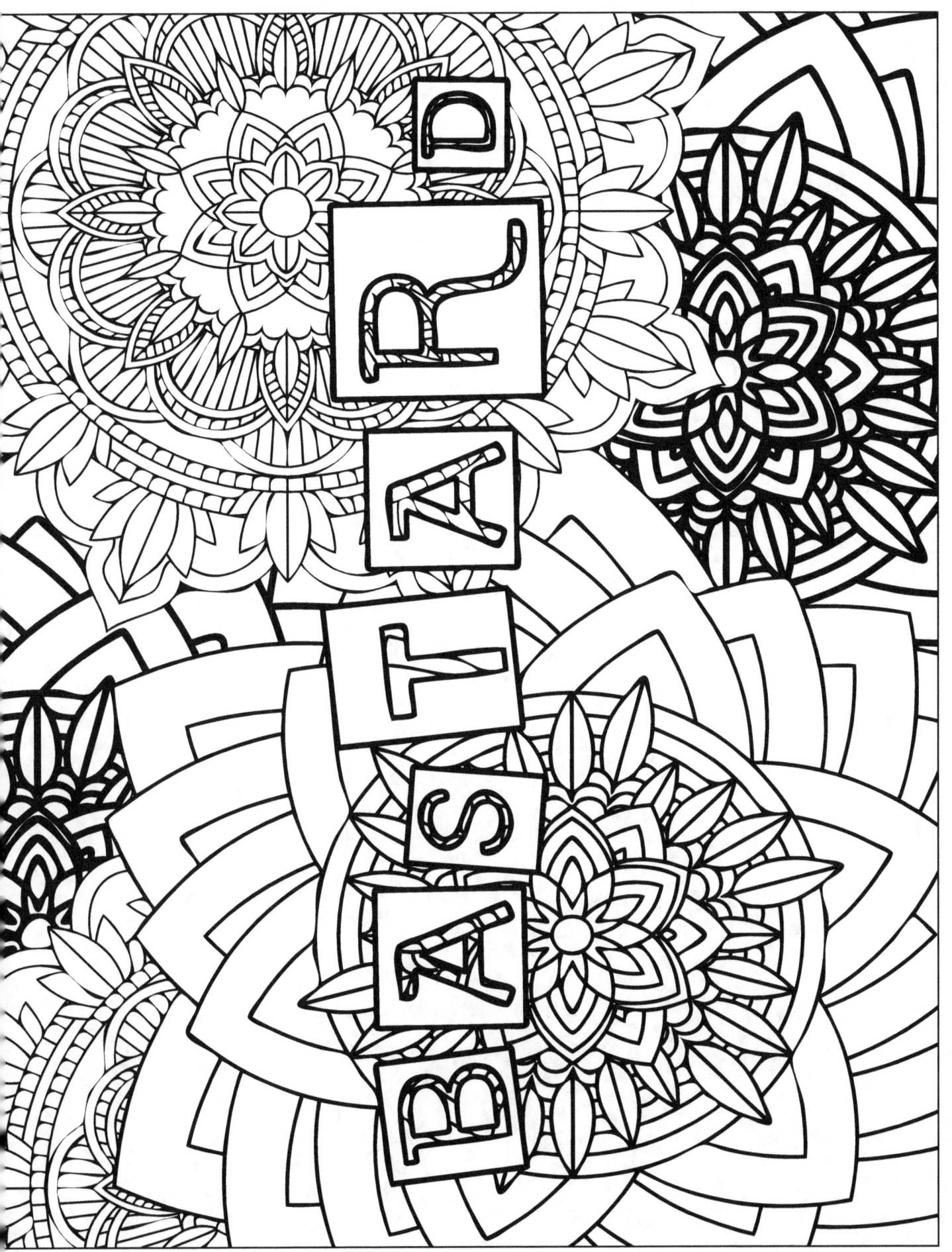

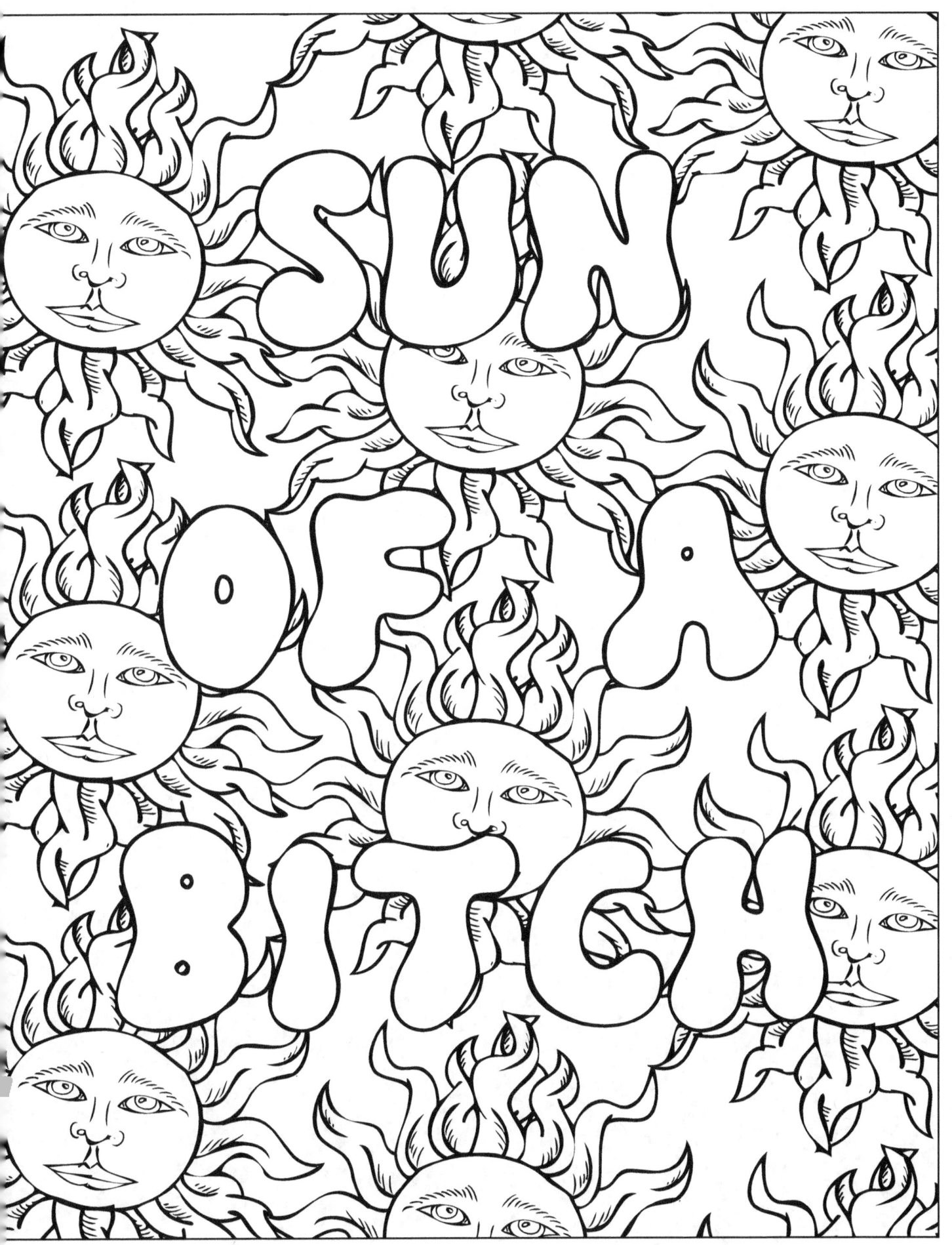

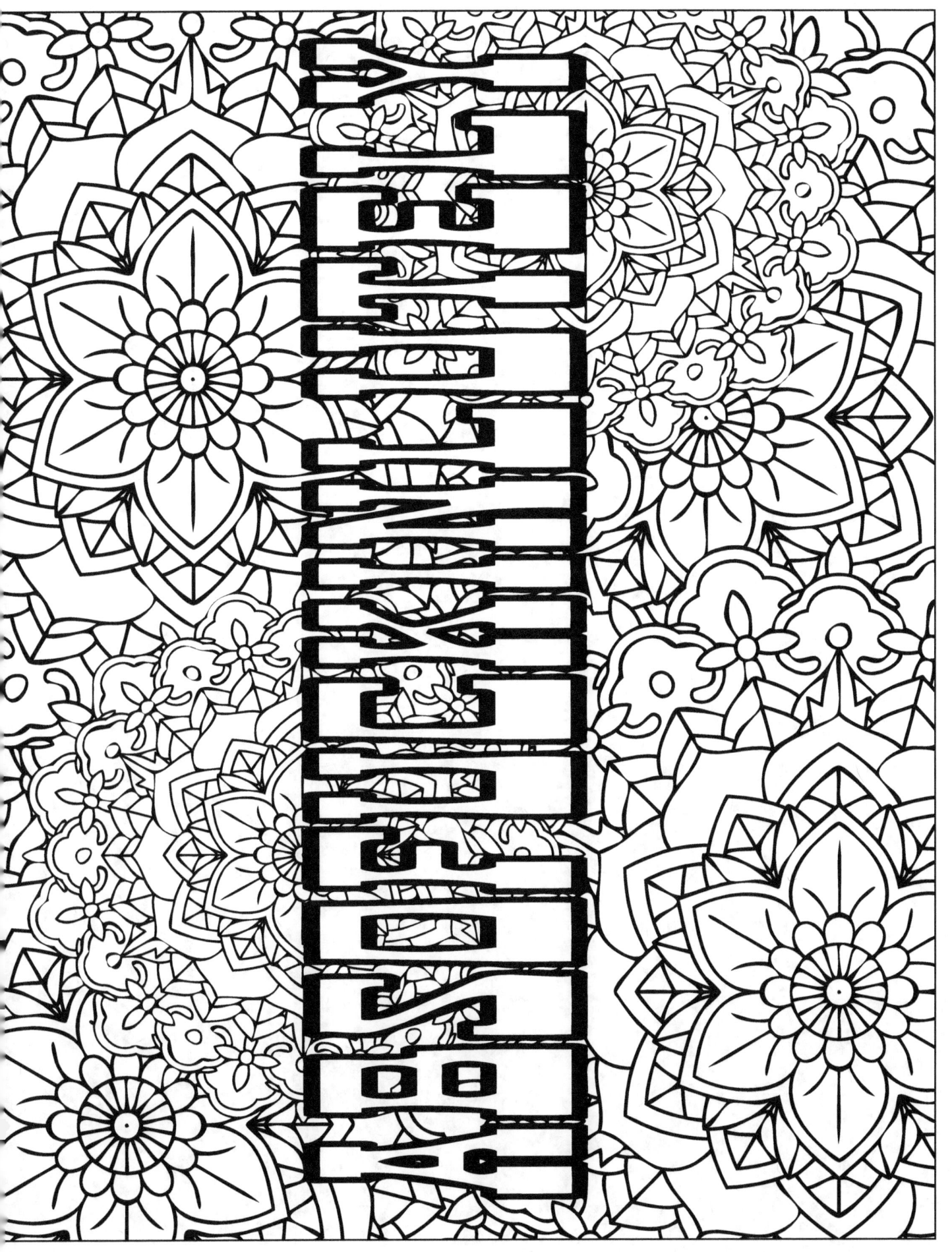

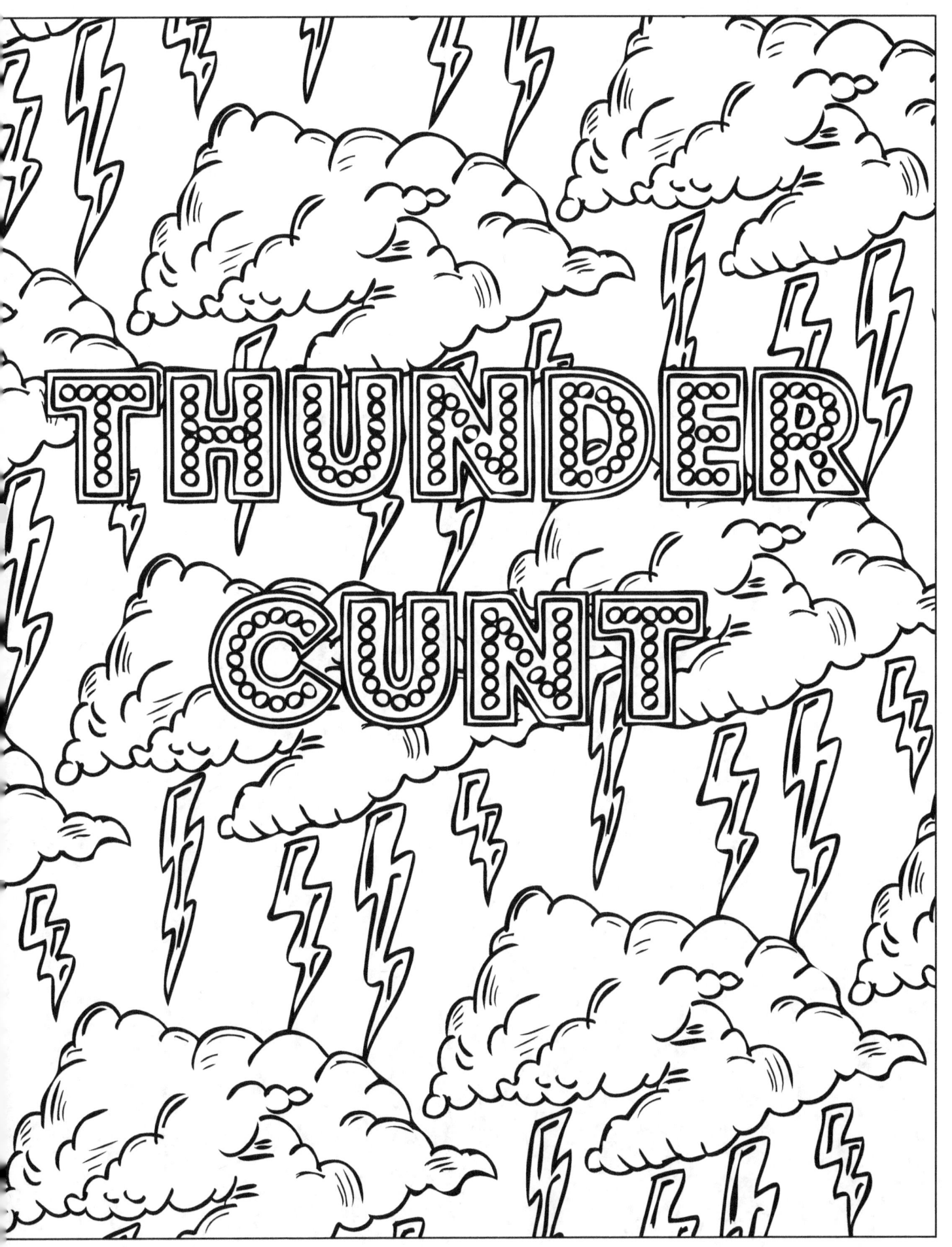

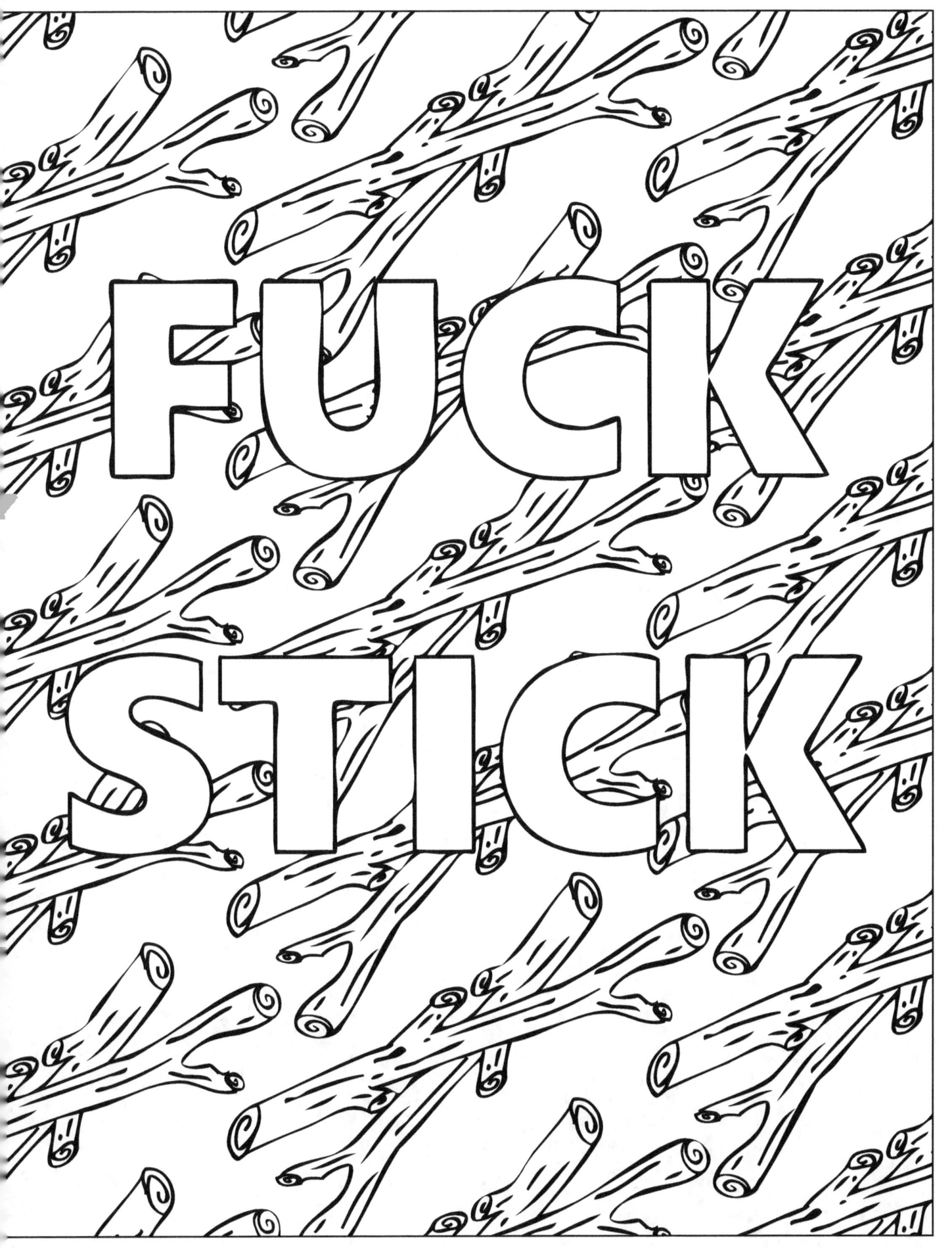

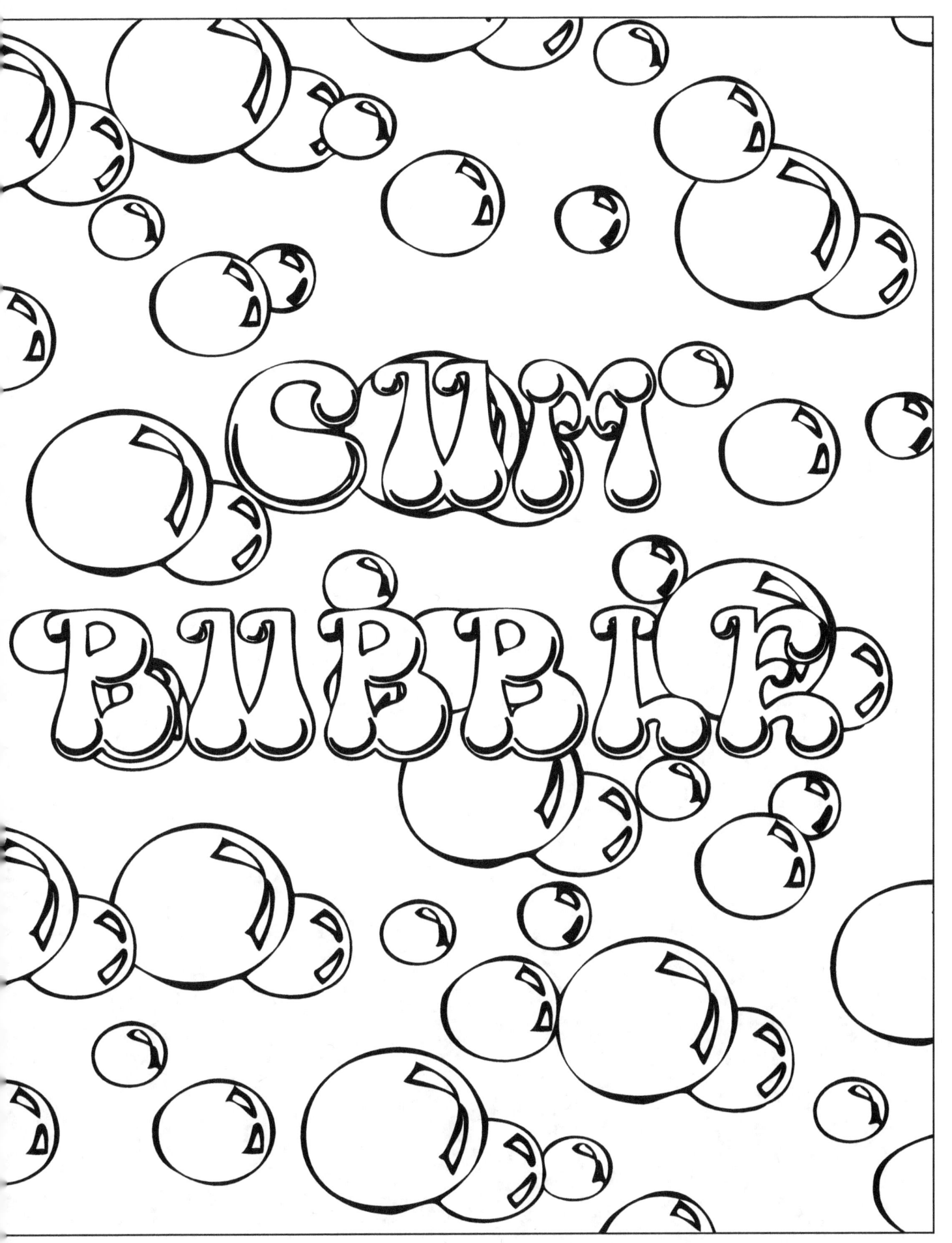

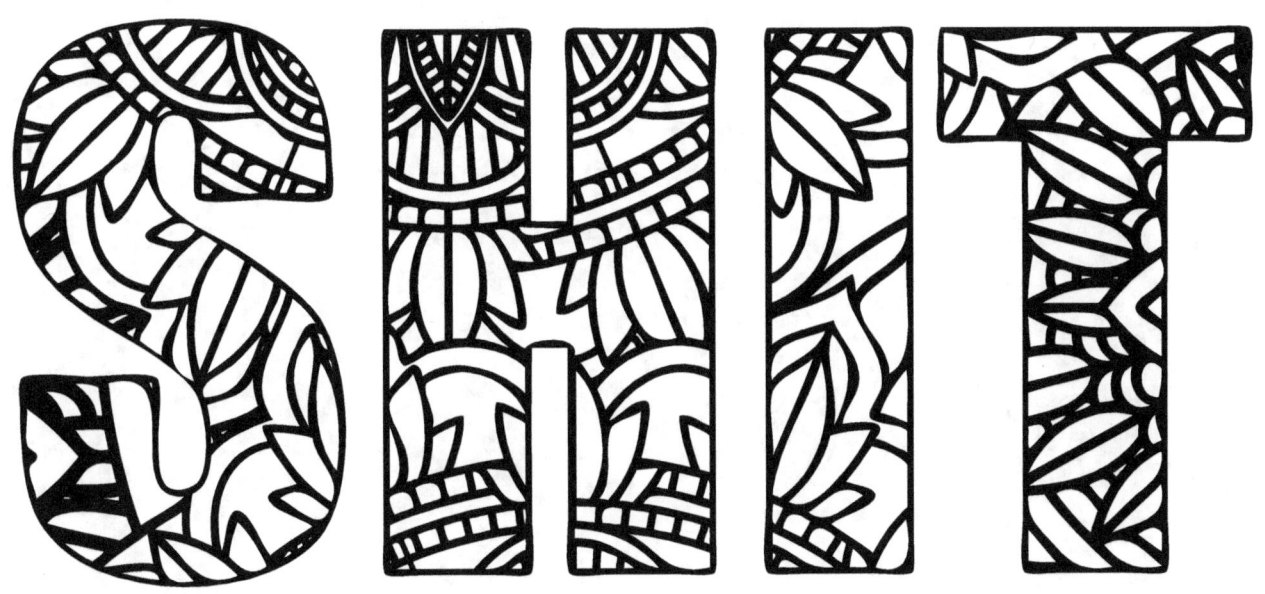

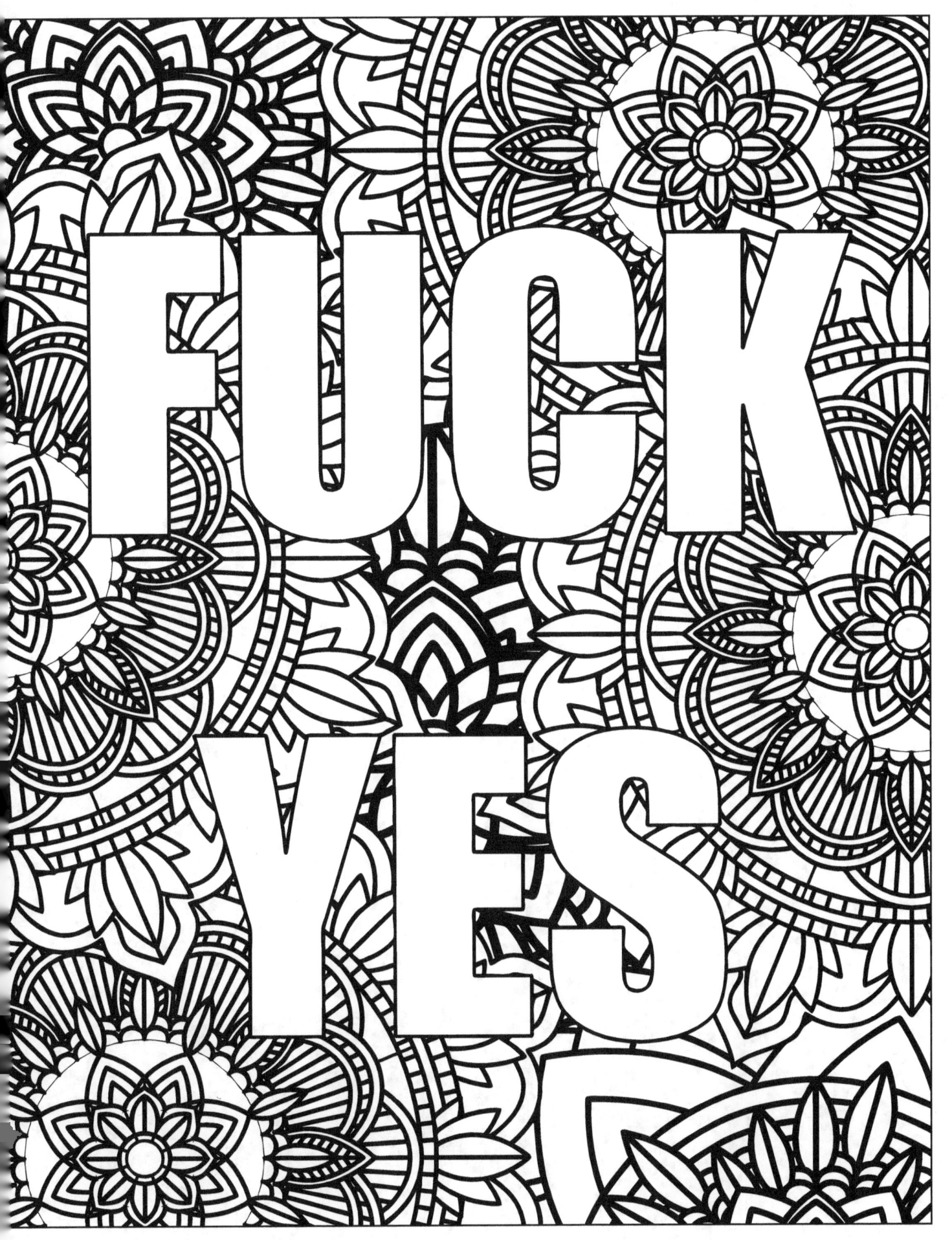

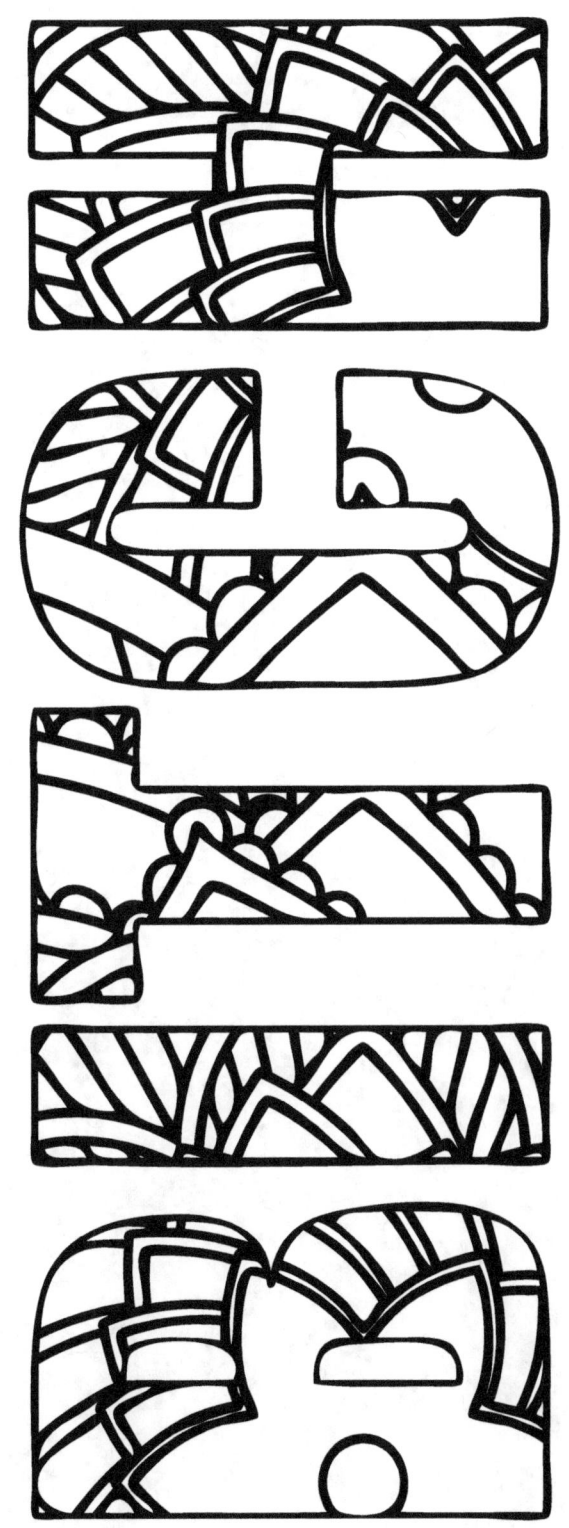

www.ingramcontent.com/pod-product-compliance
Lightning Source LLC
Chambersburg PA
CBHW081549240526
45470CB00024B/2913